Write

STARTS

Creative prompts to get you writing!

RUNNING PRESS
PHILADELPHIA · LONDON

© 2010 by Running Press
Illustrations © 2010 by Corinda Cook
All rights reserved under the Pan-American and International Copyright Conventions
Printed in the United States

9 8 7 6 5 4 3 2 1
Digit on the right indicates the number of this printing

Library of Congress Control Number: 2009920360

ISBN 978-0-7624-3569-2

Cover and interior designed and illustrated by Corinda Cook
Edited by Kristen Green Wiewora
Special thanks to Meghan Zolnay

Running Press Book Publishers
2300 Chestnut Street
Philadelphia, PA 19103-4371

Visit us on the web!
www.runningpress.com

Introduction

What makes the idea of writing so romantic? Does a novelist live inside of everyone, just waiting for the right opportunity to make himself known? Even the seasoned bestselling author needs discipline and practice to hone his craft—sometimes even more so than the novice! Whether you are a weekend poet or have a few published books under your belt, you admit you could use a little jump-start every once in a while: think of this book as the greatest writing teacher you've ever (or never) had. Train your inner writer by writing every day. Use the prompts in these pages to start a story, to rattle your brain, to stretch your limits, and to learn what you never knew lived inside your pen. Mix it up. Begin in the middle, or at the end. Record something you've never seen, never knew, or can't imagine, and make it come alive. Narrate your treasured memories or your happiest times, and mold them in a new way. You have the freedom to create something entirely new, something that has never been written before.

Get going!

Imagine you had an extra limb.
What would you do with it?

Write a story from
the perspective
of a particular room
of your house.

_____

_____

_____

_____

_____

_____

_____

_____

_____

_____

_____

_____

_____

_____

_____

_____

_____

_____

_____

_____

_____

_____

_____

_____

_____

"The best time to plan a book is while you're doing the dishes."

—*Agatha Christie*

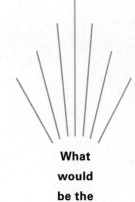

**What
would
be the
absolute
best
way
to die?**

What's your
earliest memory?

You've just been jilted at the altar.

Write what you'll do next.

DESCRIBE YOUR **WORST NIGHTMARE.**

"Two roads diverged
in a wood and I—
I took the one less traveled by . . ."

—*Robert Frost*

Choose two fictional characters from different stories you've read and create a scene in which they interact.

WRITE THE ENDING FIRST.

Imagine a challenging mental or physical handicap and write about your day from that perspective.

Write about an addiction.

Have a
conversation
with
Death.

Is it **worth it** to get even **?**

"The apple
never
falls far
from
the tree."

Describe meeting someone online.

Department store dummies have come alive!

What happens next?

What makes a bestseller?

In retrospect, it was a poor decision.

Write about someone driven to
insanity.

Describe a group of children with a piñata.
Is the piñata really filled with candy?

What recent headlines in the news have grabbed your attention? Write a script as though you were a reporter on the scene or an anchor summarizing the situation.

Write about the pleasures of home.

Describe your greatest accomplishment in life.

Step #1:

What is the most important purchase you've ever made?

Write a break-up letter.

Write a love letter.

*Write a Valentine
that you'd never actually deliver.*

Describe a **dream** you've had.

You have just
been given a
Time Machine.
Where are you
going and what
will you do once
you get there?

What was your very first date like?

You've been turned into a goldfish!
Write about your experience and how
you plan on returning to your human self.

IF YOU COULD INVENT A TOOL TO MAKE YOUR LIFE EASIER, WHAT WOULD YOU INVENT?

Write a supermarket **tabloid** article. Make it as **unbelievable** as possible.

You live in an underground city.
Write about your life.

Is it possible for an
inanimate object to
have an interesting life?
Write about the life
of a pair of scissors.

"When I Grow Up, I Want to be..."

Write a fractured fairytale.

YOU ARE IN A FOREIGN COUNTRY AND YOU
DON'T KNOW THE LANGUAGE. WHAT DO YOU
NEED TO CONVEY, AND HOW DO YOU DO IT?

Explain the furniture in your bedroom.

What is the **meaning of life?** Be deliberately vague.

Describe your first day of school.

Take a secondary character from
a favorite novel and tell
the story from that point of view.

> "Before all else,
> be armed."
>
> —*Niccolo Machiavelli*

PRETEND TO BE SOMEONE ELSE.

An
8-hour
car trip.
Break it
down.

What do your neighbors do all day?

**Take five minutes
to write in a stream
of consciousness.**

Describe a perfect vacation, and then write about how it goes wrong.

Talk about the one that got away.

Write a holiday story opening with

"Fruitcakes are not all bad."

Plan the most important
meal of your life.

Your houseplants have developed an appetite for meat.
How do you solve this problem without getting eaten?

Why do you still have that ugly shirt from 10 years ago?

CHRONICLE A DAY IN THE LIFE
OF A STREET PERFORMER.

A prison guard writes
to the parents of a
person on Death Row.

What's the **most important** thing anyone ever said to you? Did you take the advice?

Write about colored glasses.

"There is nothing more deceptive than an obvious fact."

—*Arthur Conan Doyle*

How does it feel to wear something that doesn't fit?

Create a character who is going to jail.
How did he get to this point and what happens next

Take a well-known literary character and make him or her the opposite sex. How does it change the story?

You wake up and realize that you've been sleeping for a thousand years. What is the world like now?

 Describe the most embarrassing ten minutes
that you have ever experienced.

**Look out a window
and describe what you
see in colorful detail.**

How can winning the **lottery** make life worse?

Write about being mistaken for a celebrity.

"Art is a lie that makes us realize the truth."
—Pablo Picasso

Does everything have a silver lining?

Write about a bad smell.

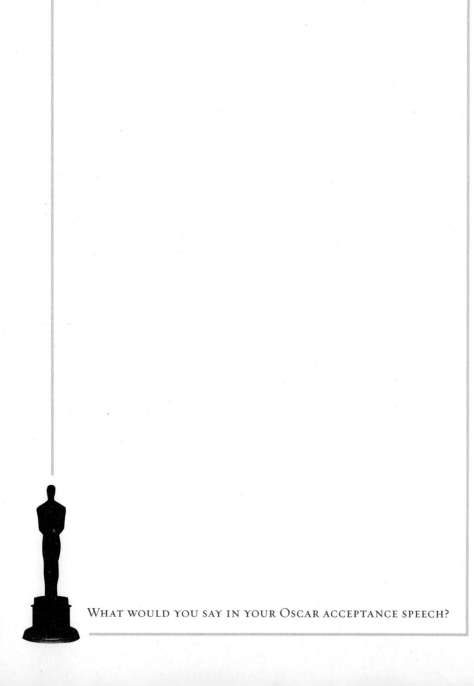

WHAT WOULD YOU SAY IN YOUR OSCAR ACCEPTANCE SPEECH?

You meet your childhood idol . . . **at rehab**.

WiSH On
STarS.

Is the cup half-empty or half-full? Why?

Describe a perfect day.

Think of the most diabolical villain, and then write a scene where he or she is doing something utterly mundane in a very particular way.

"Be obscure
clearly."

—*E.B. White*

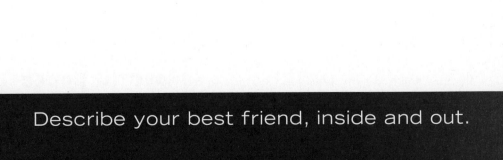

Describe your best friend, inside and out.

Imagine you had a machine you could use to create **world peace** against the will of the people. What would happen if you used it?

Create a biographical
sketch of the
next stranger you see.

Imagine star-crossed lovers who meet tragic ends.
Now write the scene where they first meet.

An ambulance just rushed by, **SIRENS BLARING.**
Describe what's going on inside.

"ART IS AN ATTEMPT TO INTEGRATE EVIL."

—*Simone de Beauvoir*

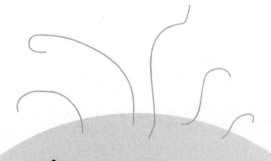

Describe going bald.

Write your own personal ad.

_____
_____
_____
_____
_____
_____
_____
_____
_____
_____
_____
_____

Now write it seriously.

_____
_____
_____
_____
_____
_____
_____
_____
_____
_____
_____
_____
_____
_____
_____
_____

Create a scene
where important
things are said
without dialogue.

Write about the first snow of the season.

You just killed your family.
Write about how you hide the evidence.

What do you see in the mirror?

**Four roommates
share a bathroom.
Hilarity ensues.**

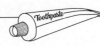

WHAT IS SO THRILLING ABOUT DRIVING FAST?

Someone has hurt you.
SPEW.

What is the importance of being earnest?

Are all bloggers writers?
How are they different?_

Throw a stone from your glass house.

> "Metaphors have a way of holding the most truth in the least space."
>
> —*Orson Scott Card*

Write about being
home for the holidays.

You've been chosen to give the
commencement speech
at your old school. It must be at
least twenty minutes long.

Write your own eulogy.
Who would deliver it?

Of whom are *you* the *most resentful?*
Who is resentful of you?

Think back to your very first love.
What would your life be like
if you were with that person now?

**What is the best comeback
that you never said in time?**

A five-year old asks you,
"Where do babies come from?"

As I watched it go spinning down the drain, I realized what a fool I'd been to be handling something so precious.

Think
of the one
person
you
absolutely
can't
stand.
Now
write his
death
scene.

What's on page 317 of your autobiography?

"NOBODY HAS EVER MEASURED,
NOT EVEN POETS,
HOW MUCH THE HEART CAN HOLD."

—*Zelda Fitzgerald*

What's in your fridge? Why?

A BOTTLE WASHES UP THE BEACH
IN FRONT OF YOU.
WHAT DOES THE MESSAGE SAY?

If you were granted an **interview with God,**
what questions would you ask, and why?

Could you have chosen a different life?

What was the moment that you chose the path you took?

"And the first rude sketch that the world had seen
was joy to his mighty heart,
till the Devil whispered behind the leaves
'It's pretty, but is it Art?'"

—*Rudyard Kipling*

Write the last page of the novel you haven't begun.

The End

Will you ever write that novel? Why or why not?

Draft a rough will.

**DESCRIBE
A DREADFUL
KISS.**

Trace a fictional genealogical line.
Make it intersect with your own.

Is life getting harder?

Describe the most complete sense
of accomplishment you've ever had.